Edaville USA
South Carver, MA
Souvenir Book

Copyright © 2016 Debi DiCarlo. All Rights Reserved.

ISBN: 978-1-943201-10-5

All rights reserved. No part of this book may be reproduced or transmitted in any form or by any means, electronic or mechanical, including photocopying, recording, or by any information storage and retrieval system, without permission in writing from the publisher or author.

First published by AM Ink Publishing, 07/01/2016

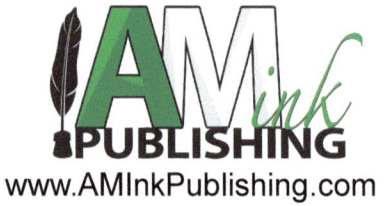

www.AMInkPublishing.com

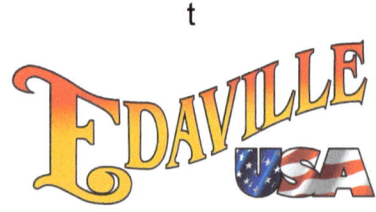

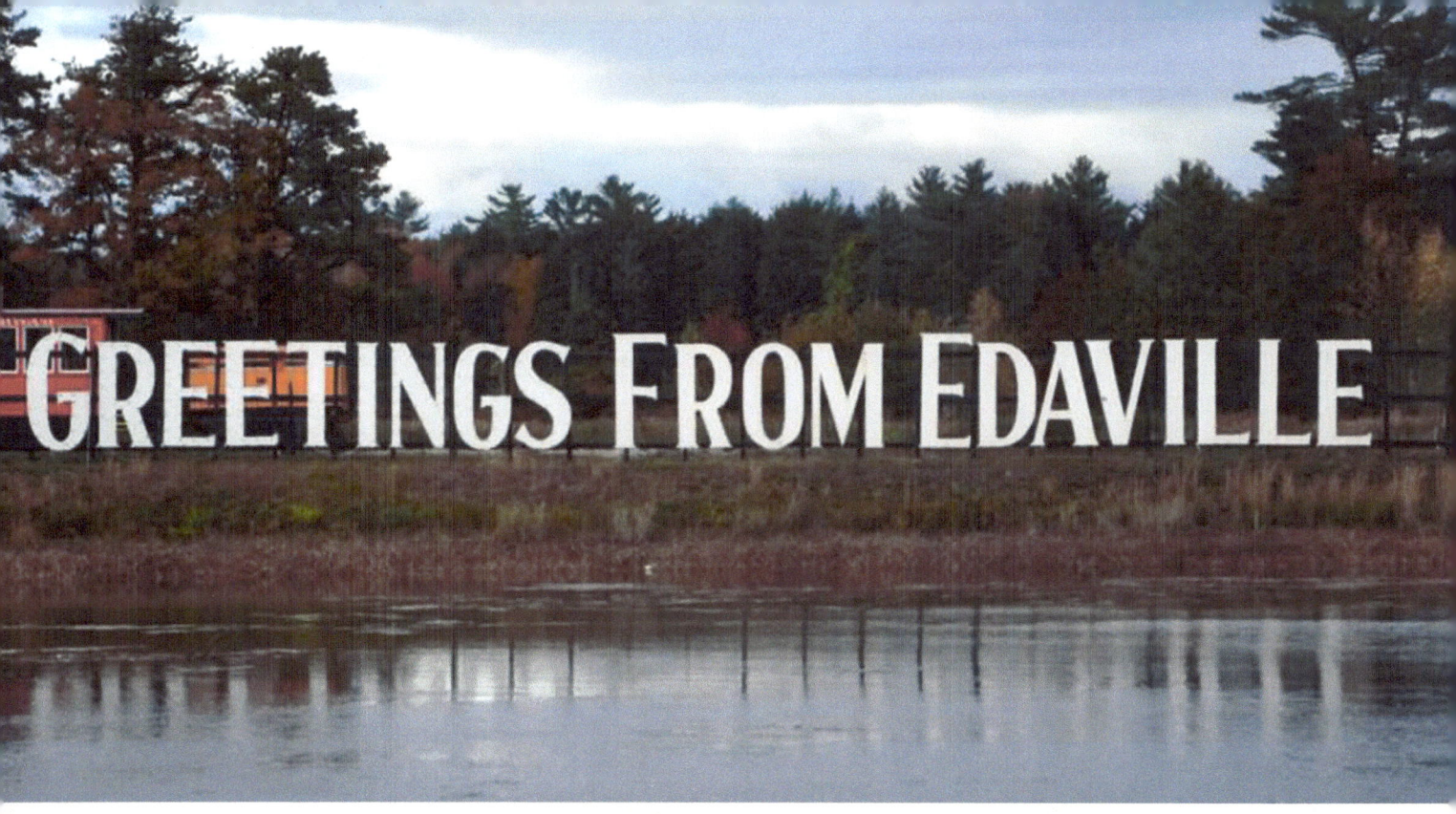

Established in 1947

Where the good times keep on rollin'...

In the 1940's, Ellis D. Atwood (EDA) acquired Maine's last working two-foot gauge railroad. This included five and a half miles of track which he set up to haul sand and berries on his cranberry bog route. He even had to add passenger cars for the over 10 million passengers that visited!

EDA named a train after his wife, Althea.

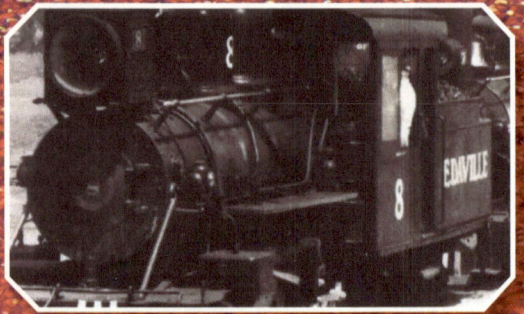

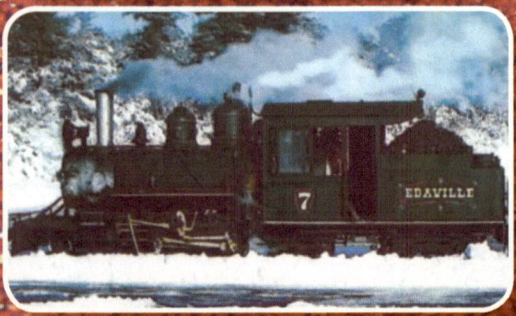

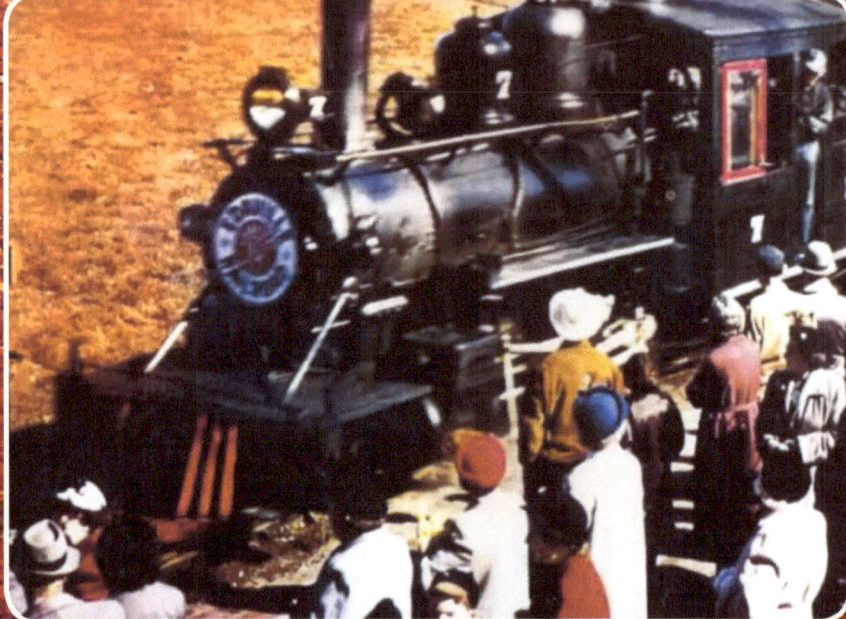

Cranberry Season

Mr. Atwood was a very successful cranberry grower. At one time, he held the largest privately owned bog in the world, 210 acres. He was a generous man who cared about his community. He built a baseball field with night lights on his property and also provided the Carver team with transportation and equipment. When he died in 1950, he was working with M. L. Urann and John C. Makepeace to organize Ocean Spray.

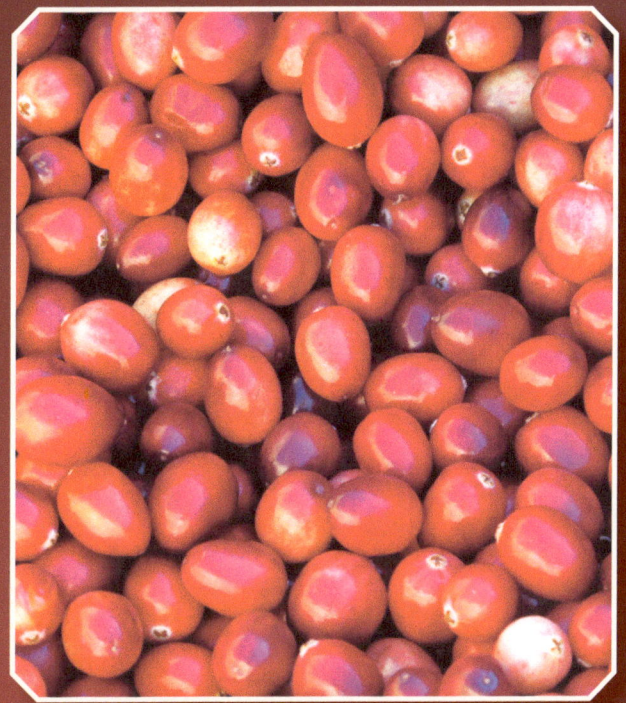

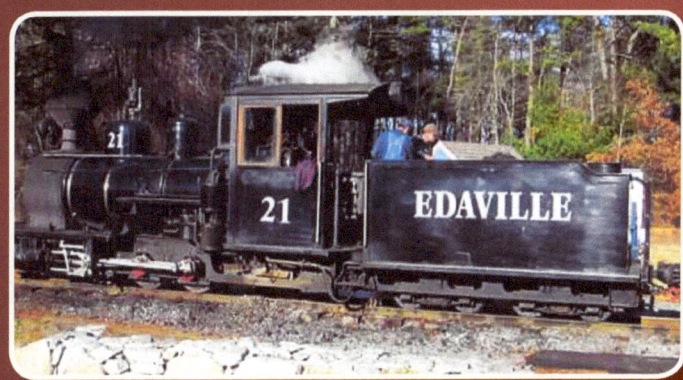

Edaville represents a by-gone way of life. The two-foot gauge railroad reflects a proud heritage. Edaville has an appeal as being something beyond simple nuts and bolts. It is determined to keep on going and preserve the total atmosphere which bring visitors back time and again. So come on down, purchase a ticket, board a wooden steamcar and listen for the conductor's cry of, "All Aboooard!!"

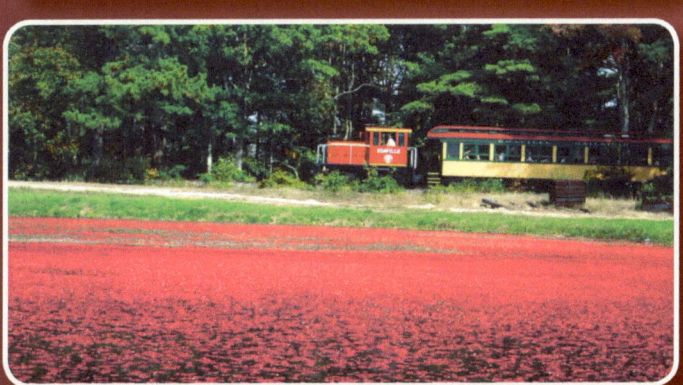

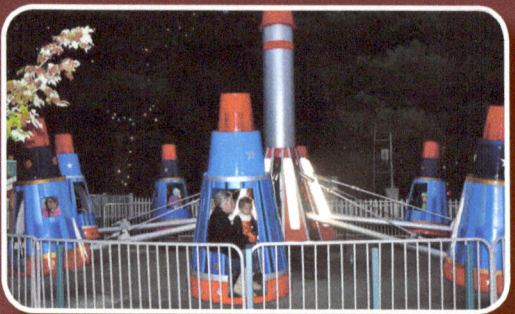
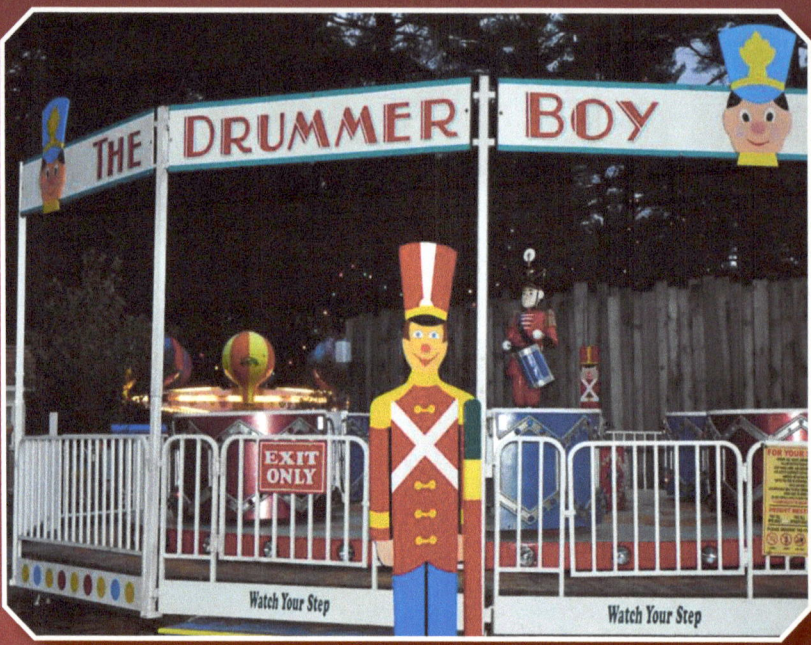
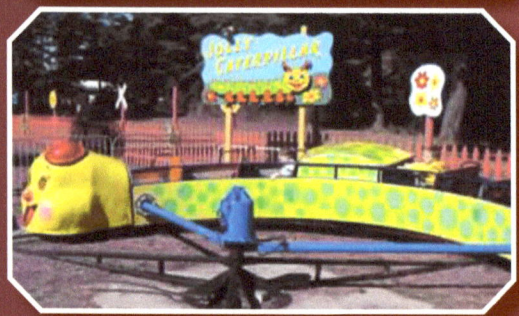

Edaville has over 90 rides and attractions!

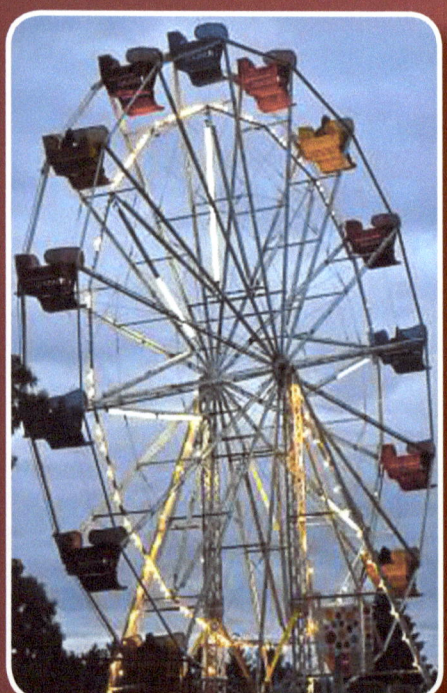
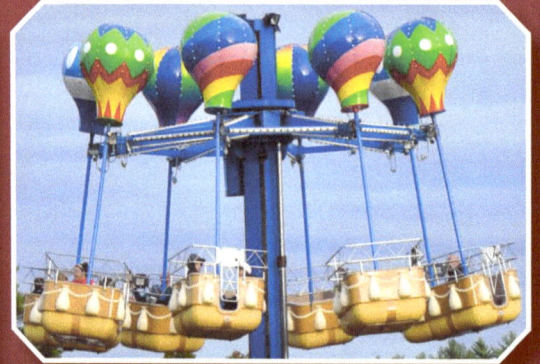
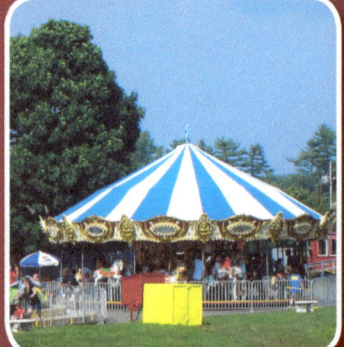
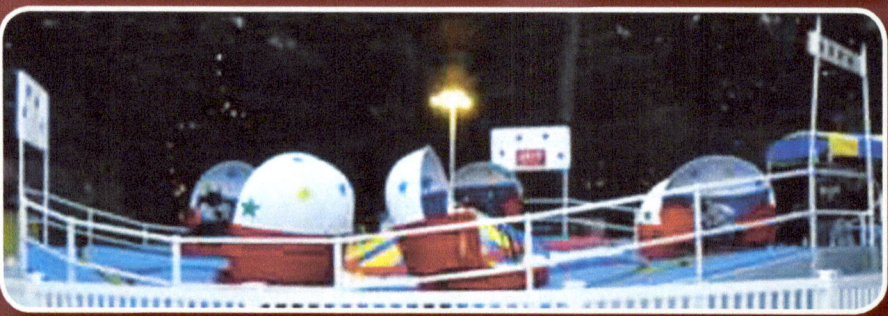

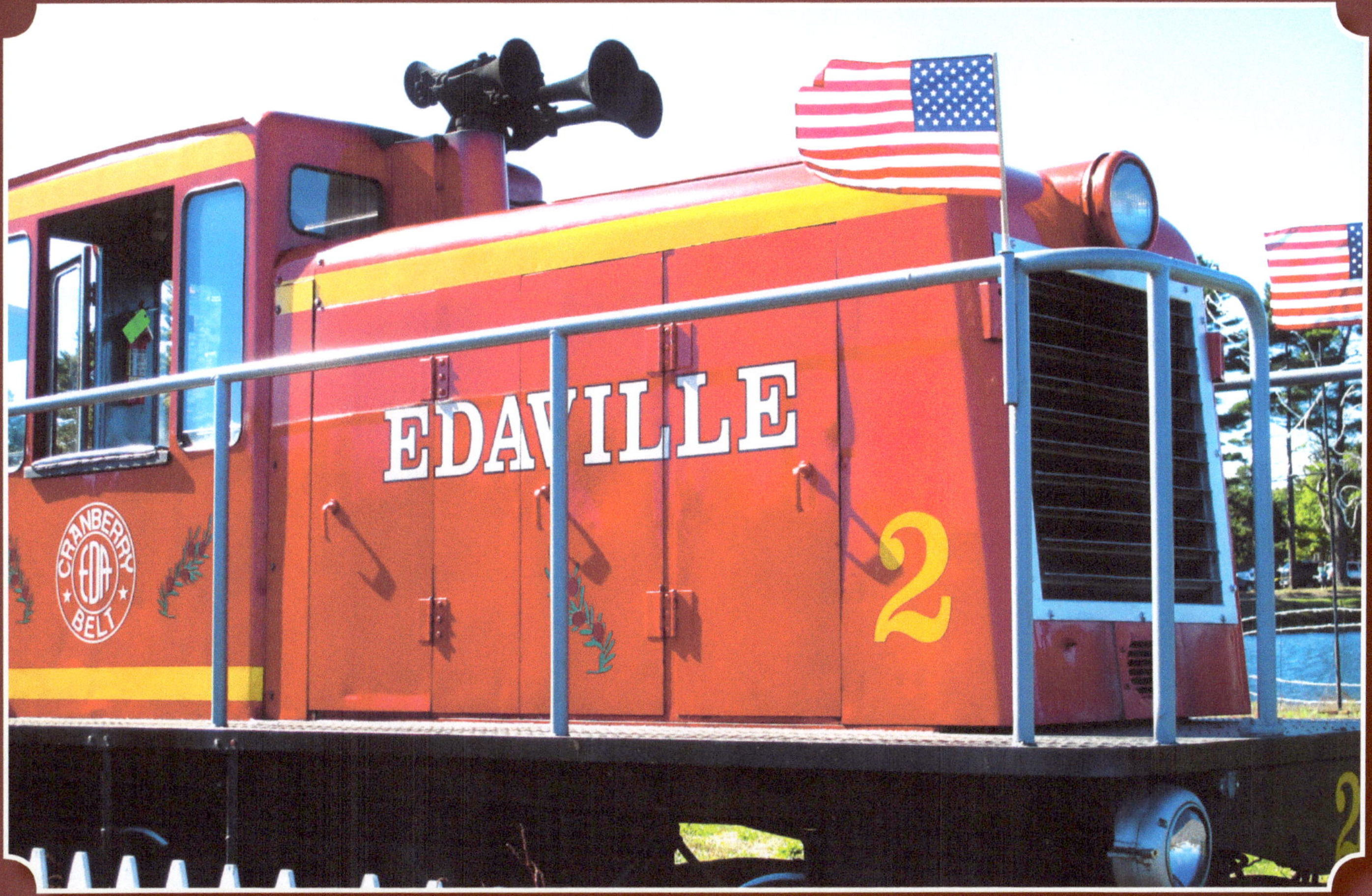

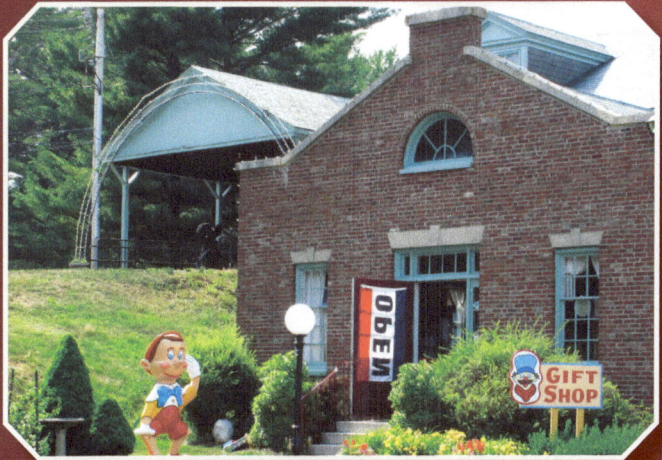
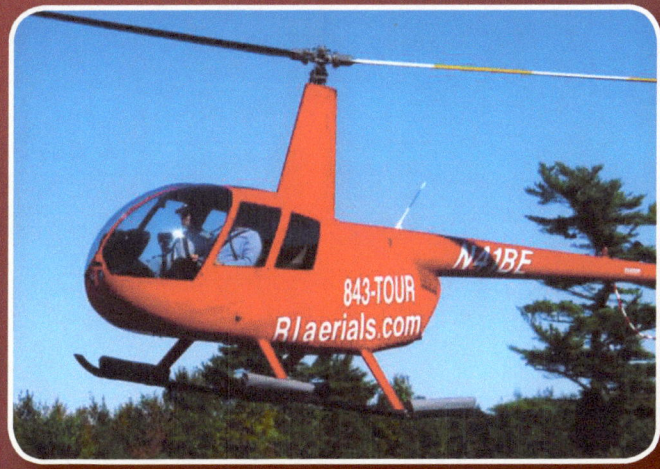

Dinoland

Dinoland is a scenic woodland trail that allows you to take a self-guided tour past 23 life-like dinosaurs!

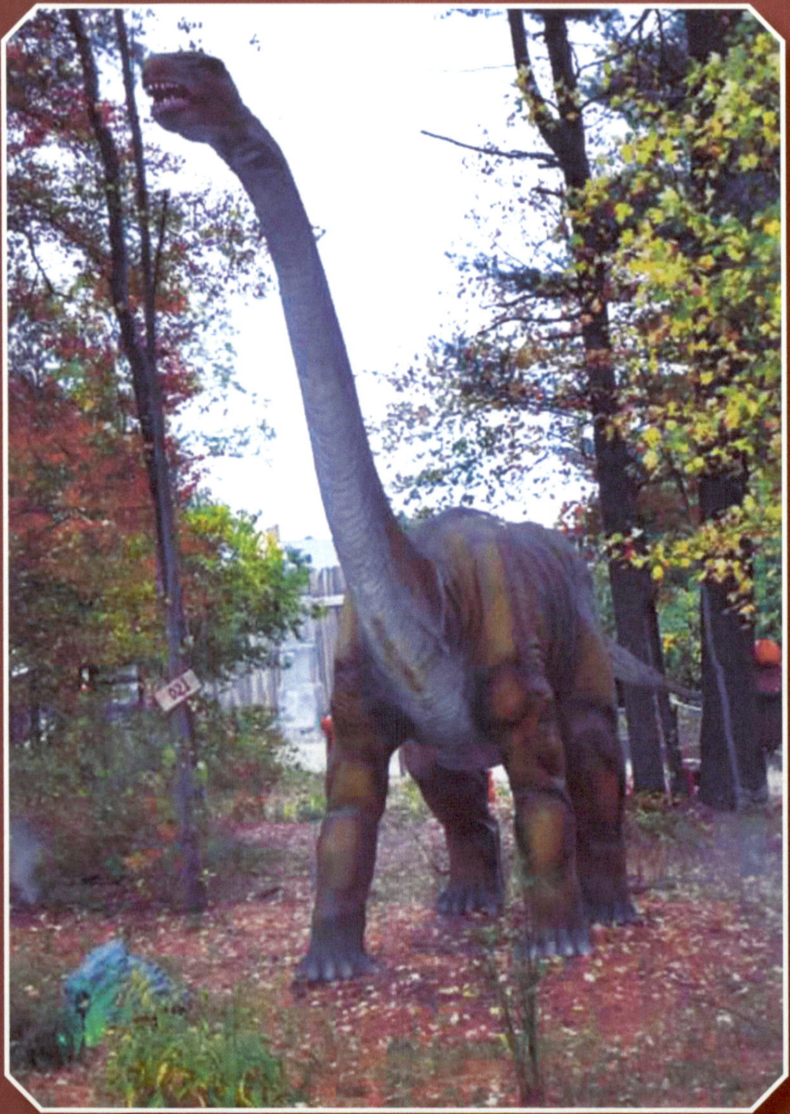

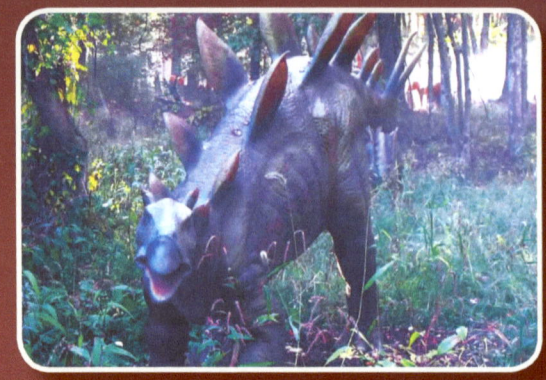
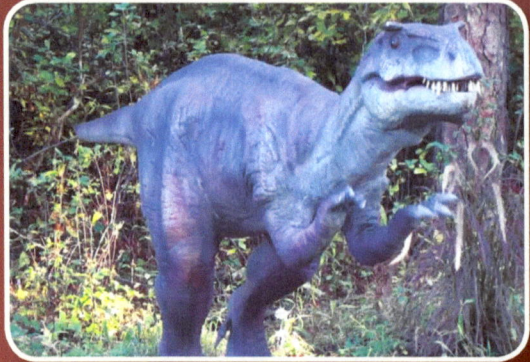
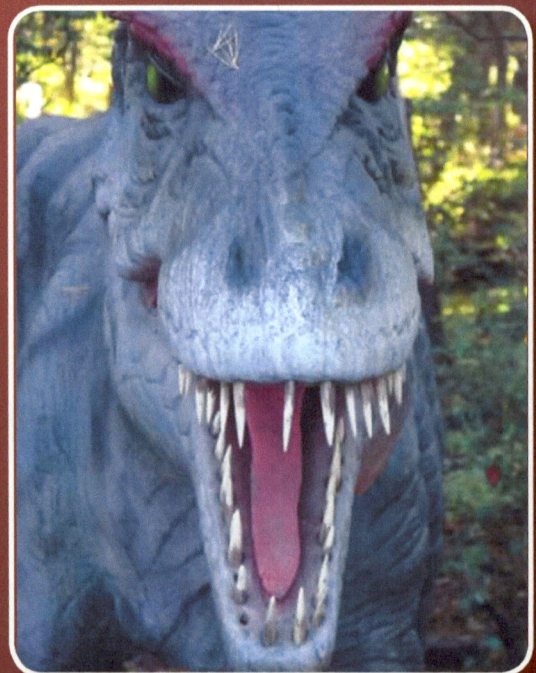

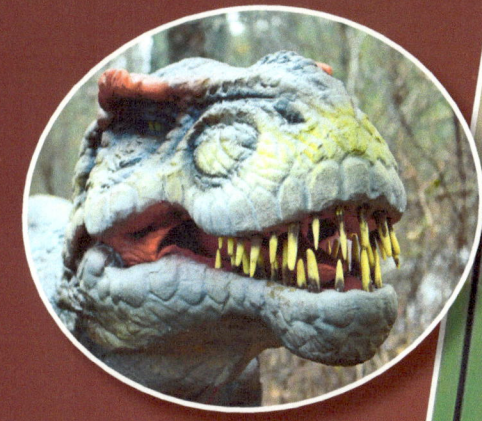
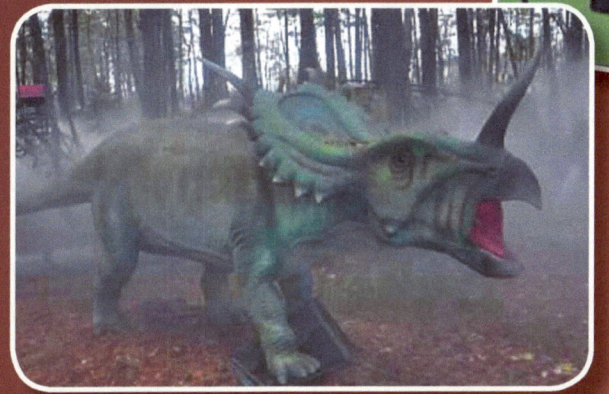
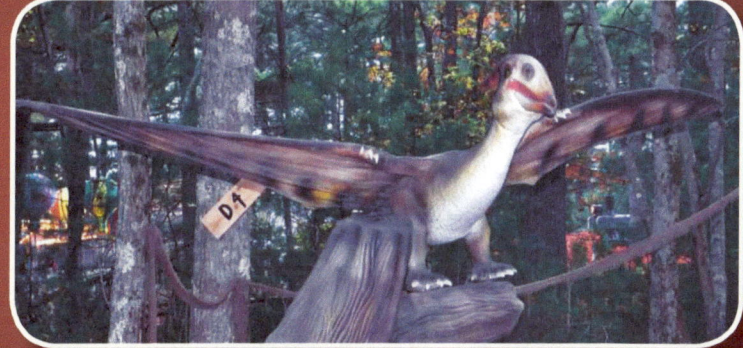
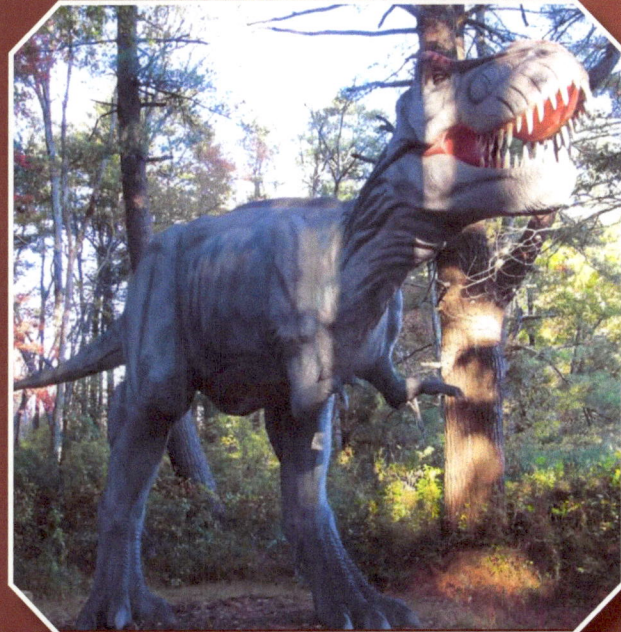
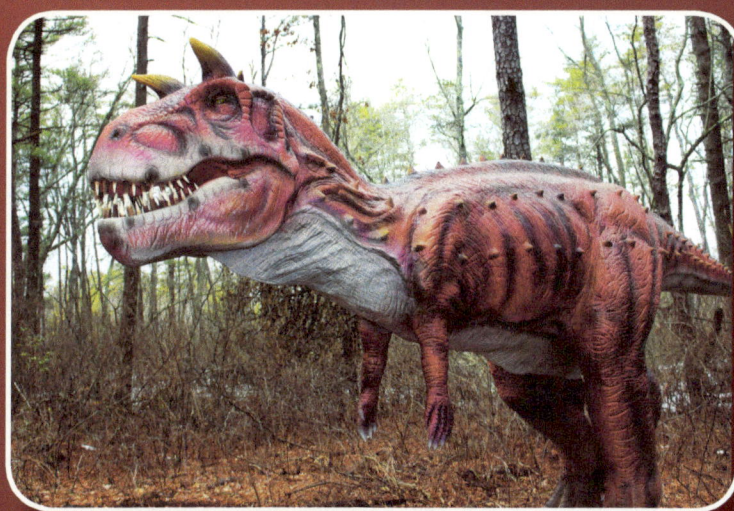

Family FUN for *Everyone!*

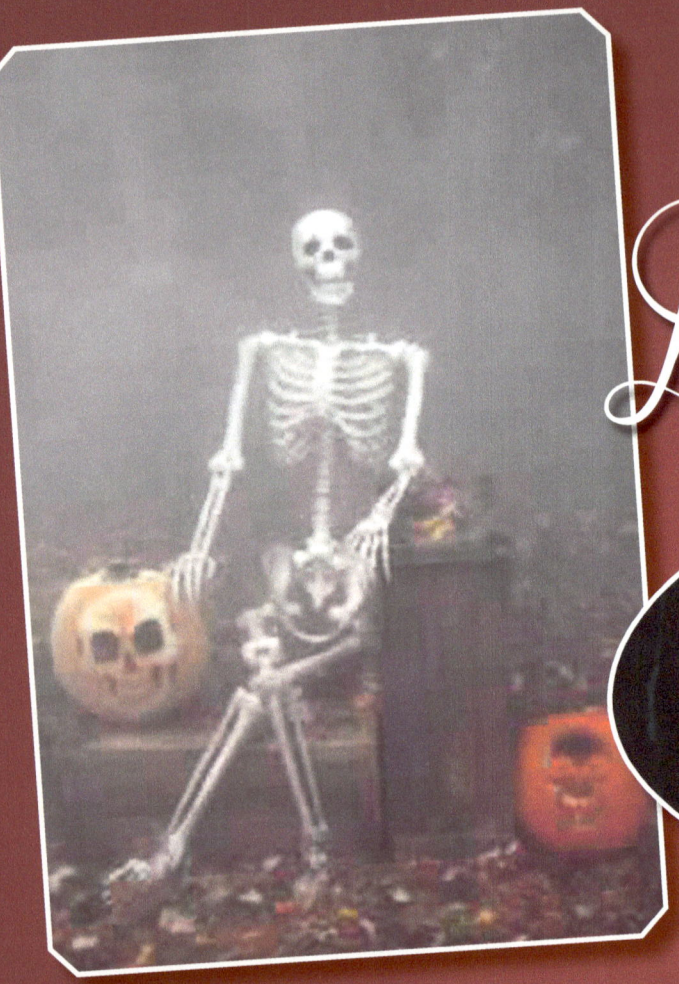
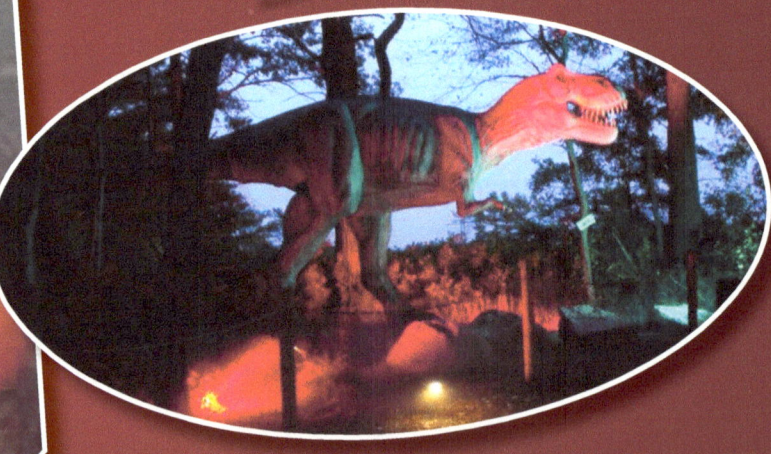
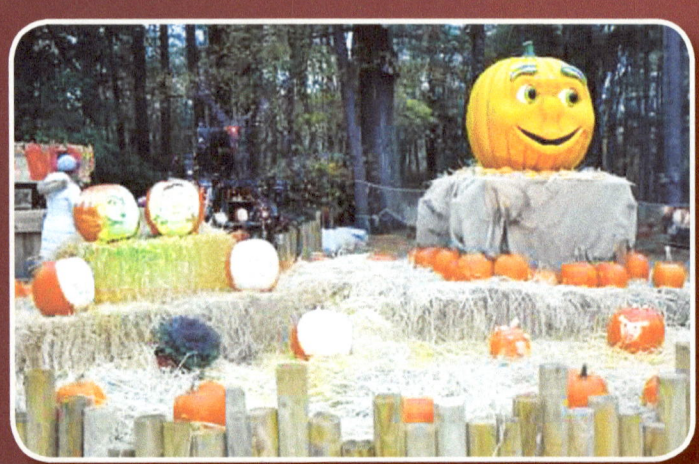
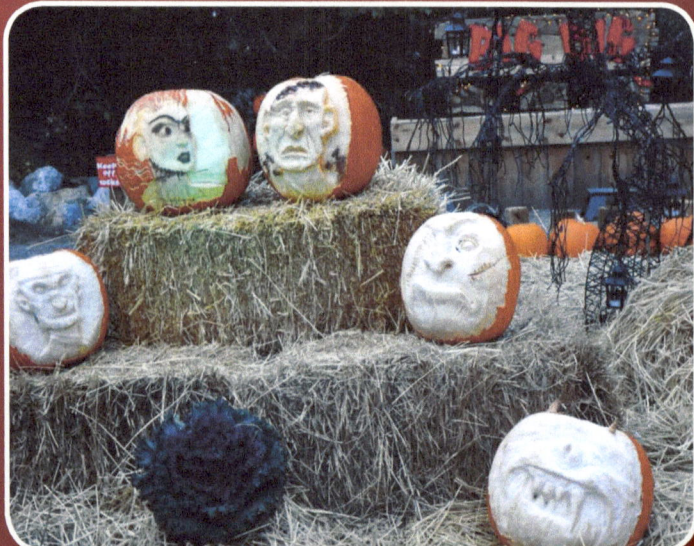

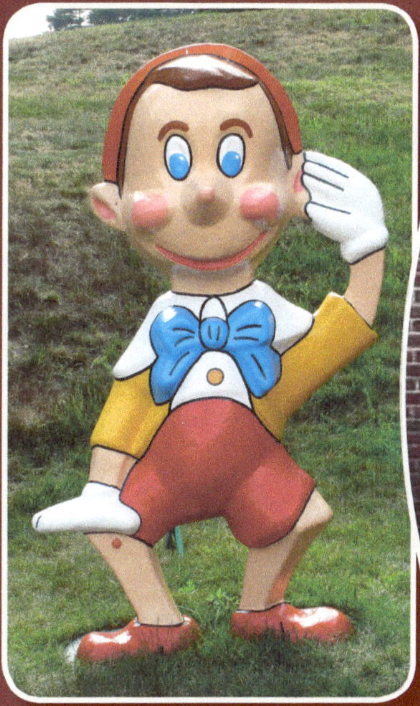

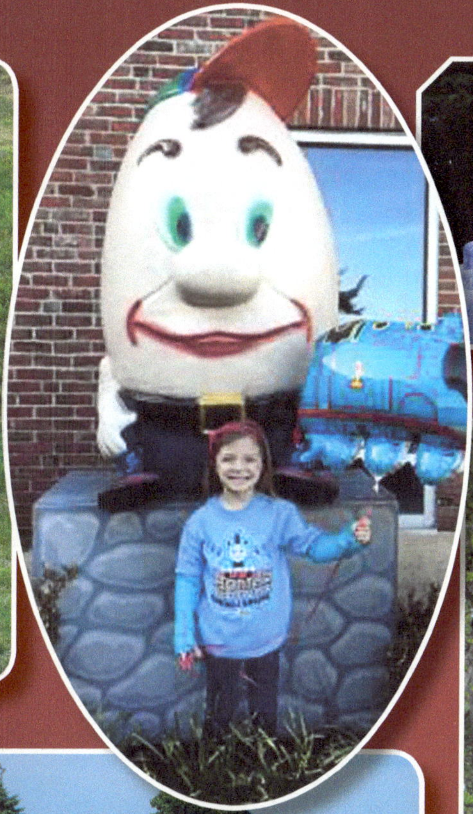

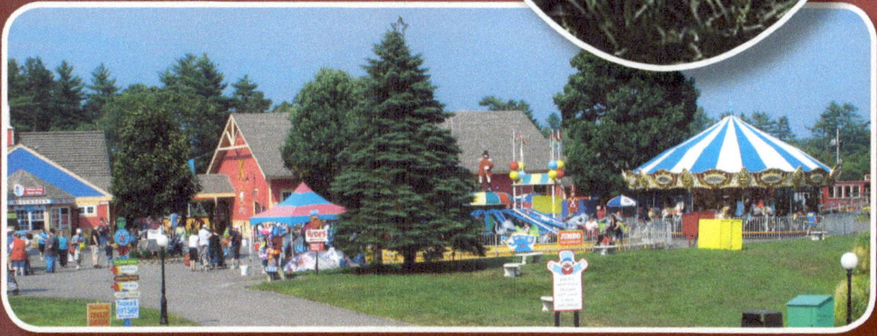

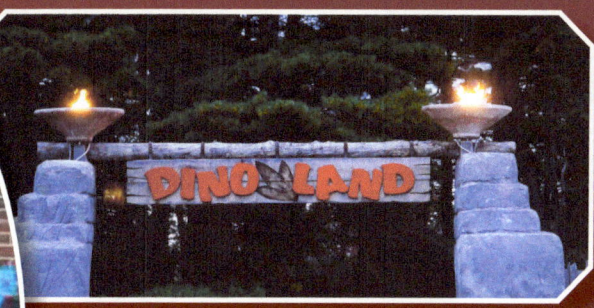
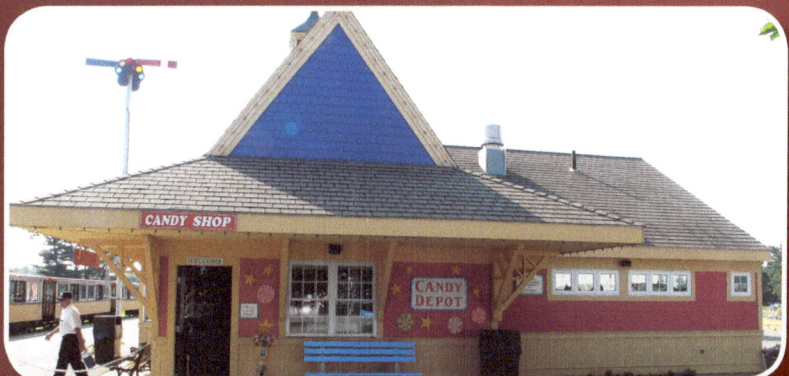
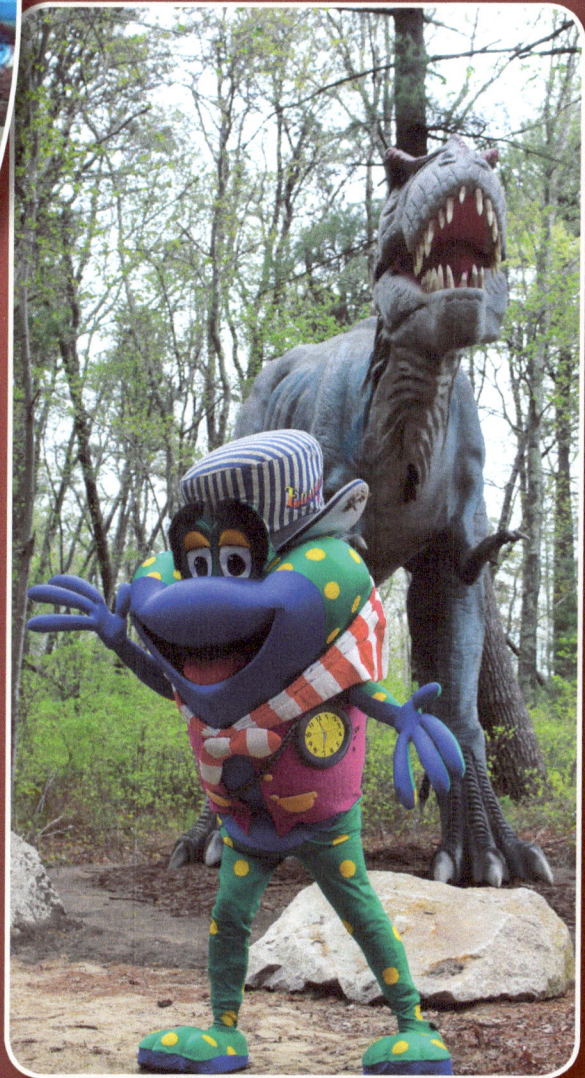

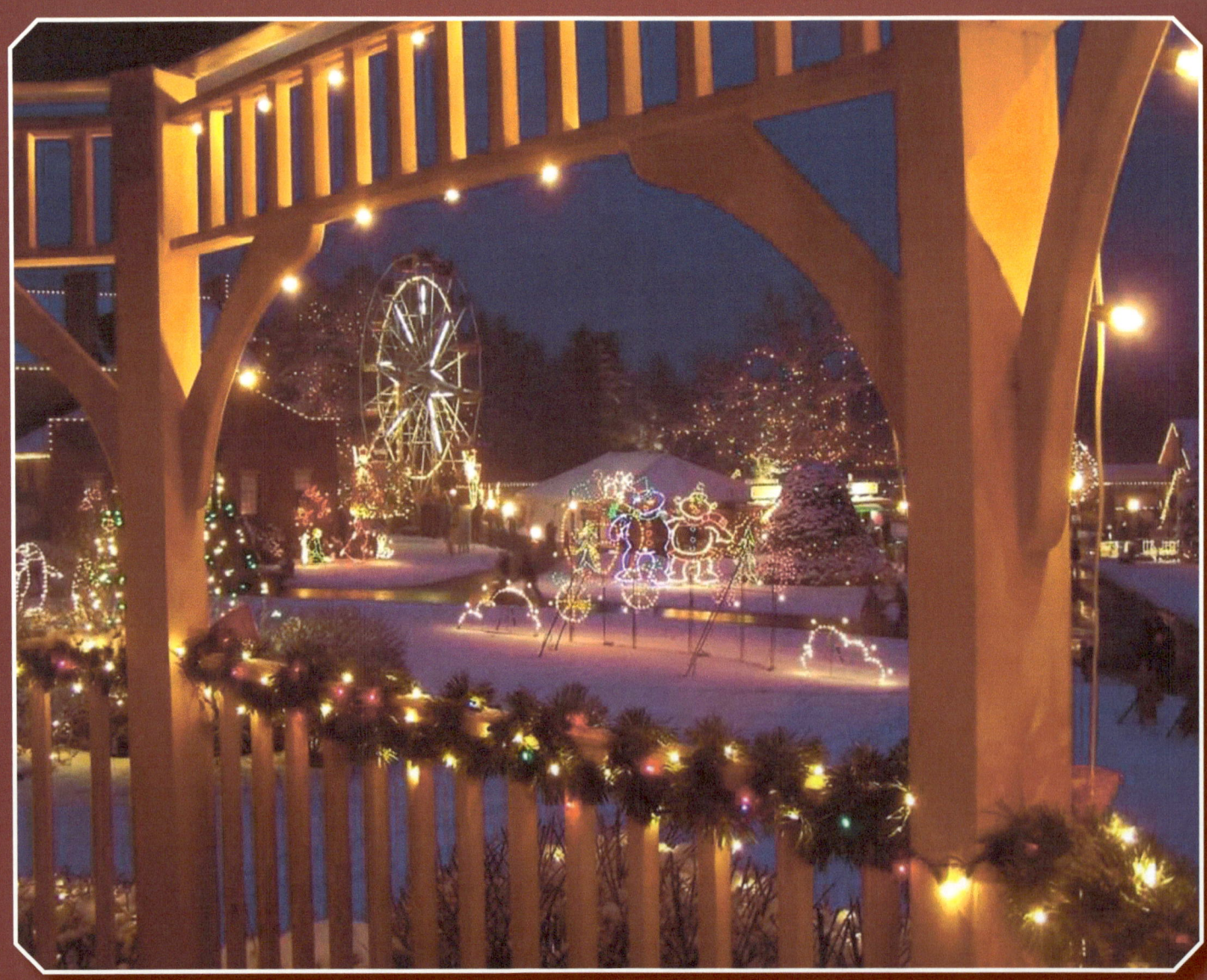

Festival of Lights

Experience the magical Festival of Lights at Edaville! Millions of lights, Santa Claus, hot chocolate, fried dough and SO MANY rides which are even open in the winter! Mr. Atwood brought all of his own Christmas exhibits to Edaville in 1947 from his home in South Carver. When he died in a sudden accident, the Festival of Lights was continued in his memory.

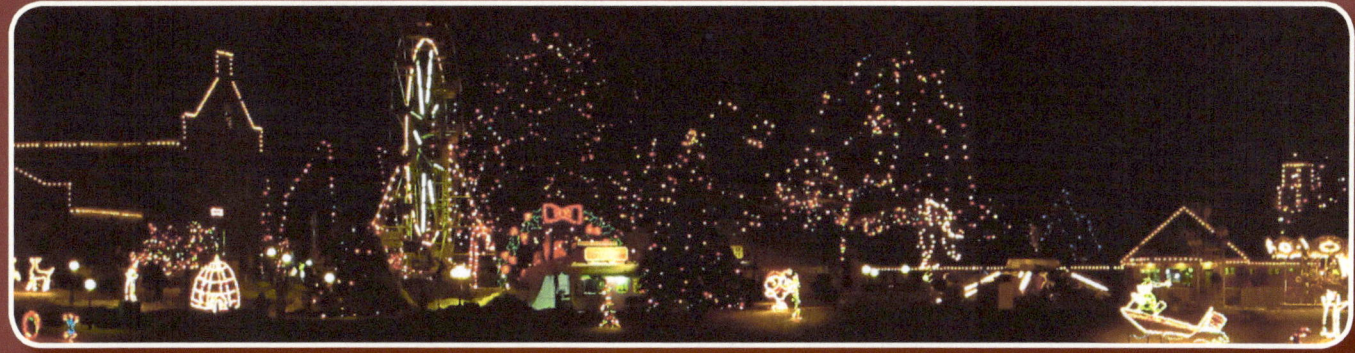

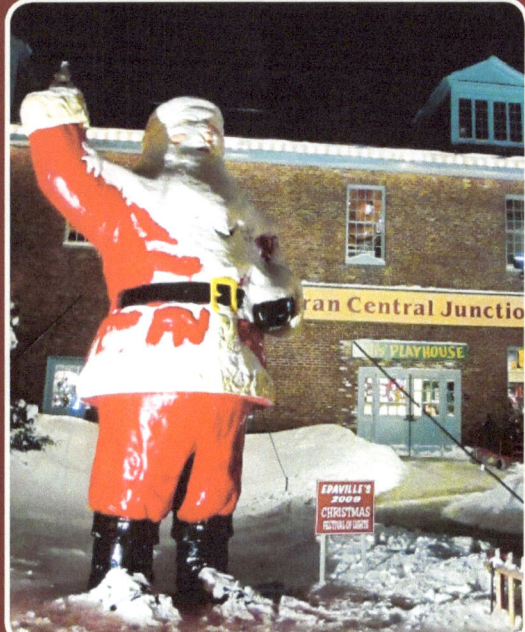

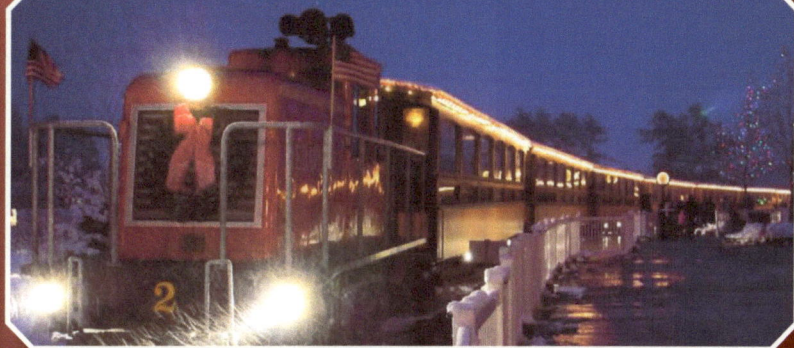

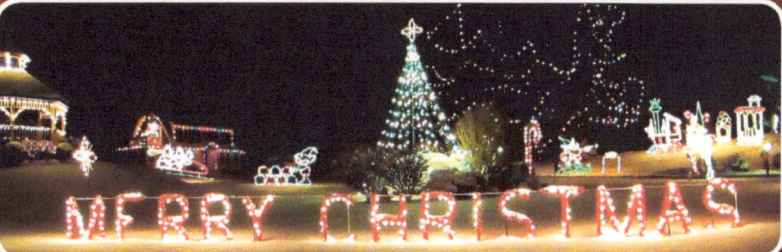

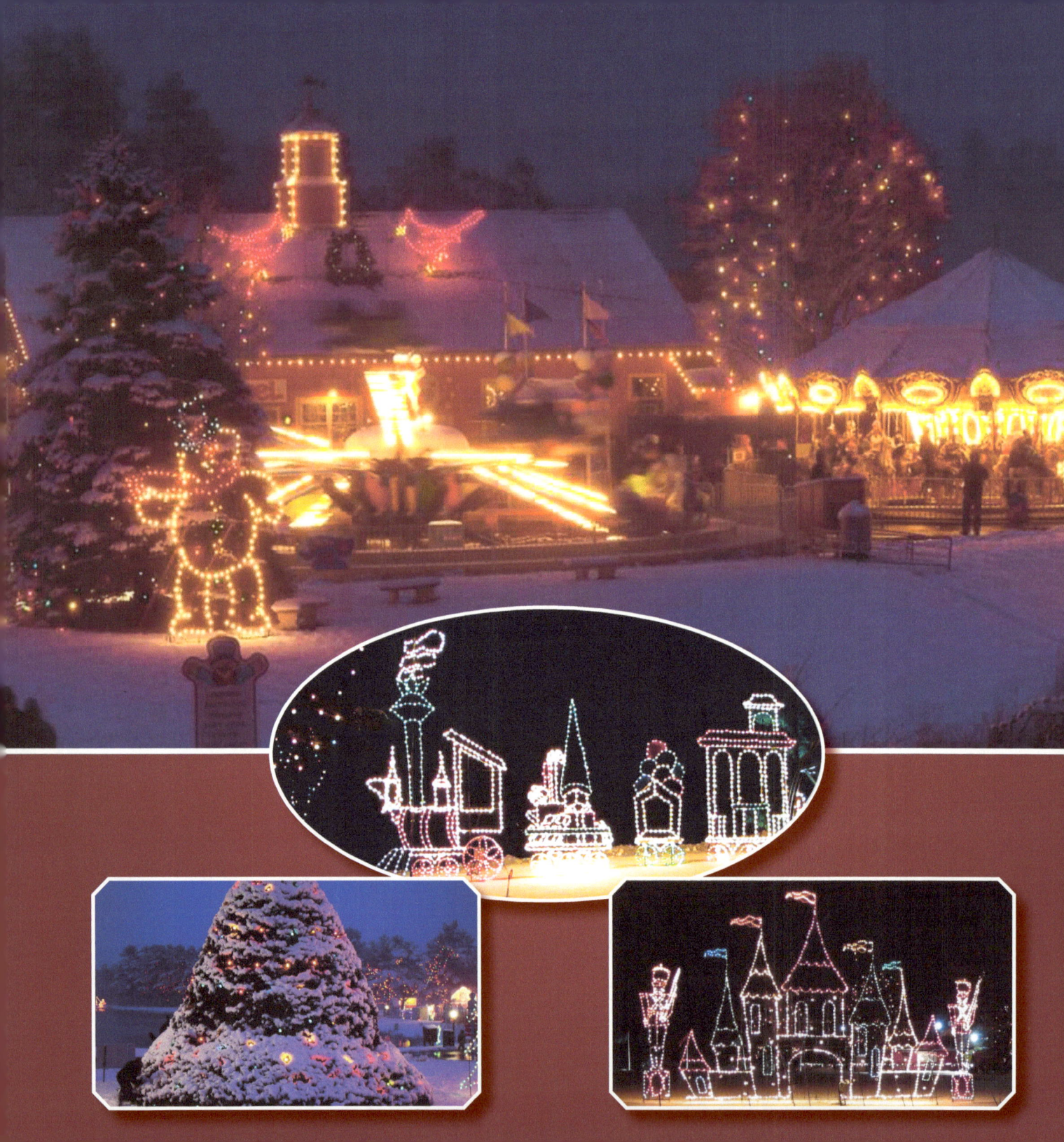

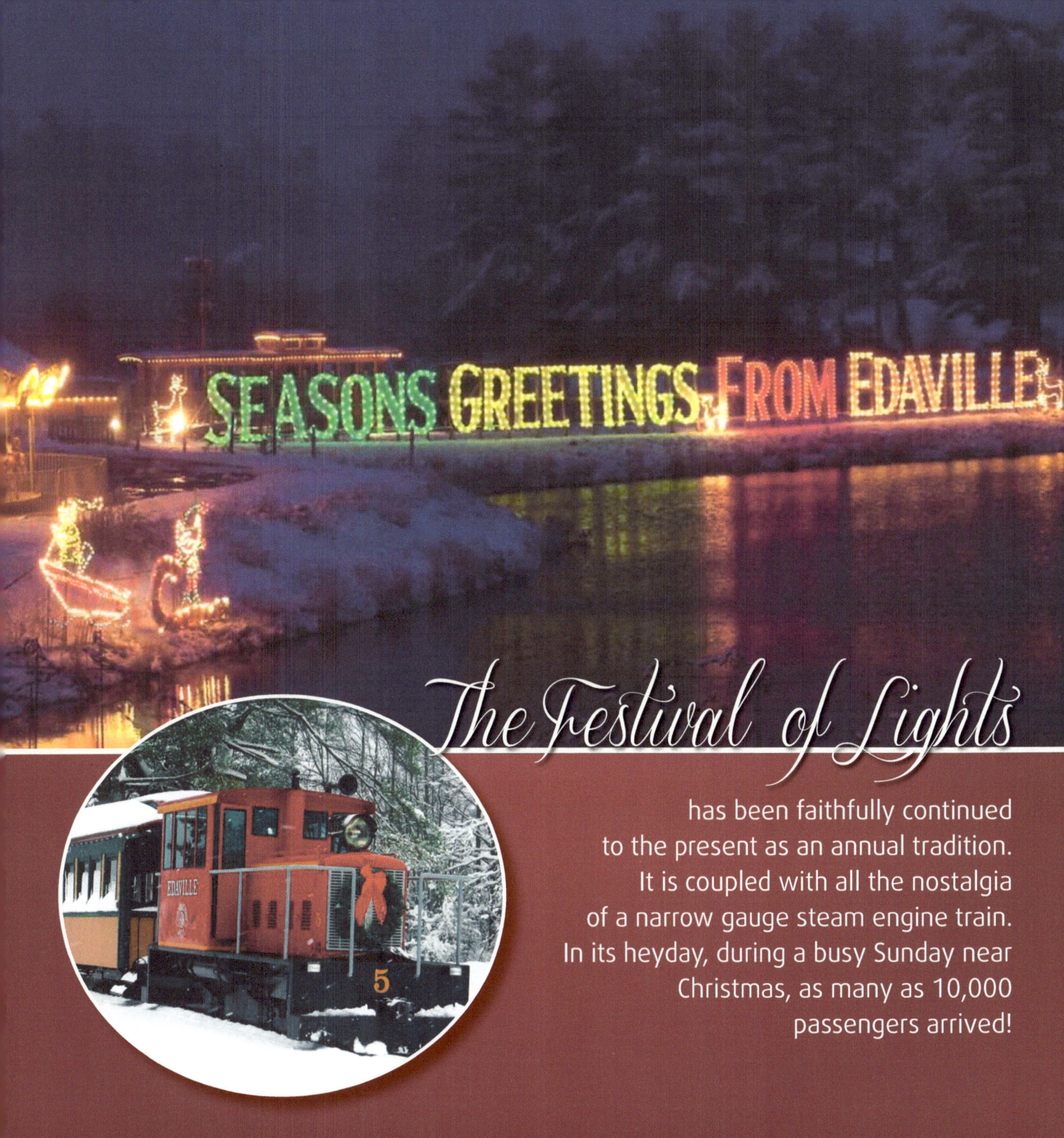

The Festival of Lights

has been faithfully continued to the present as an annual tradition. It is coupled with all the nostalgia of a narrow gauge steam engine train. In its heyday, during a busy Sunday near Christmas, as many as 10,000 passengers arrived!

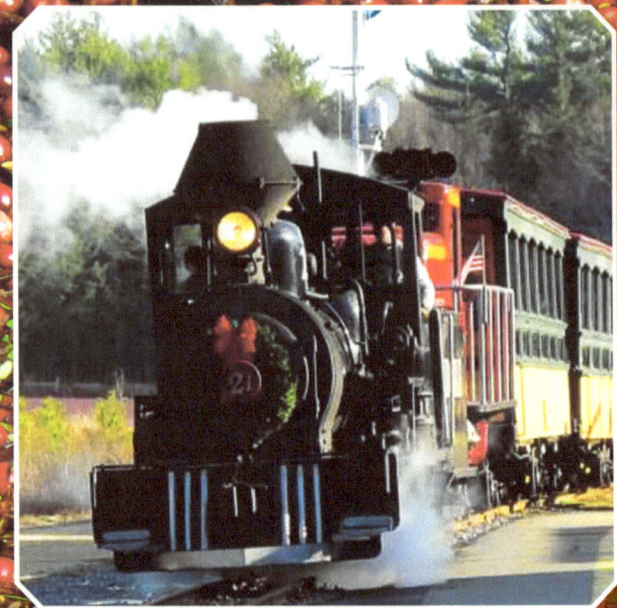
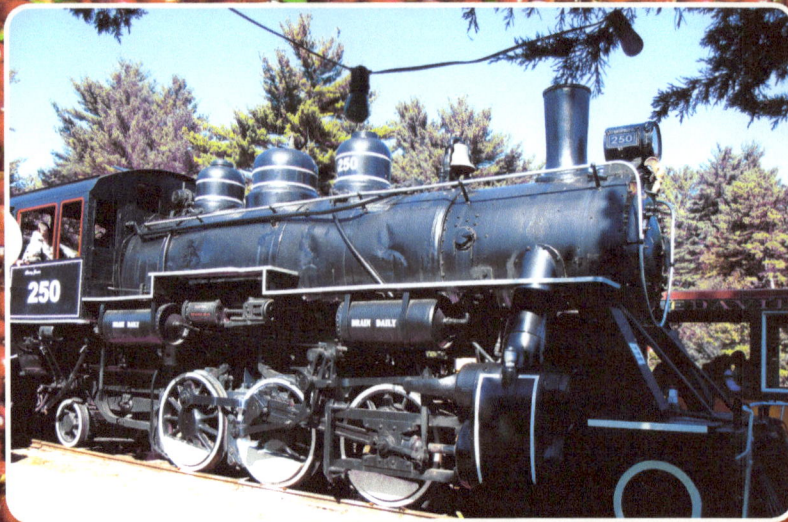
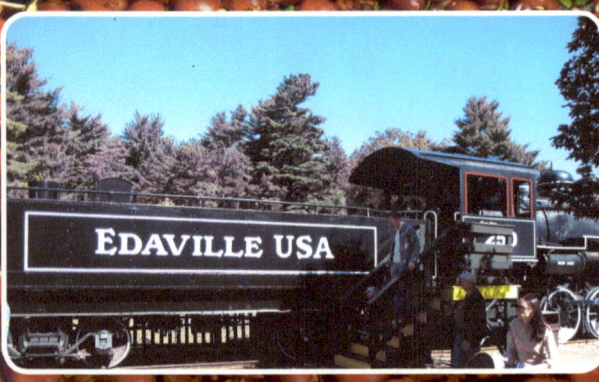
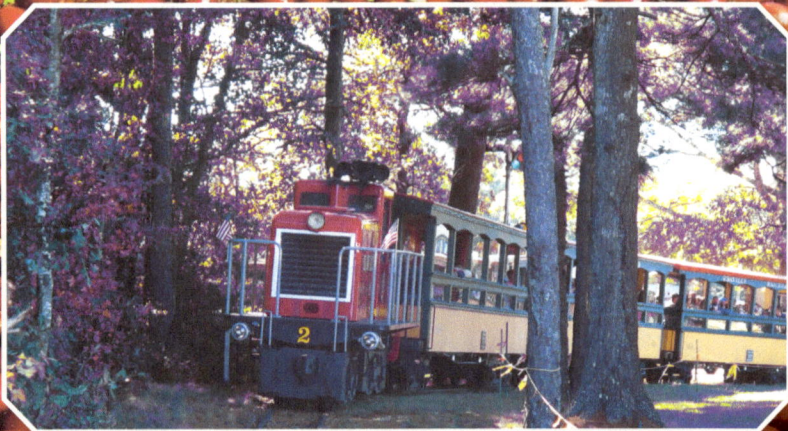
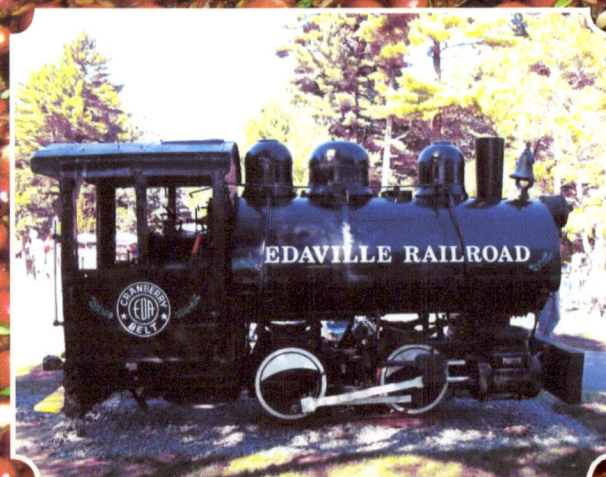
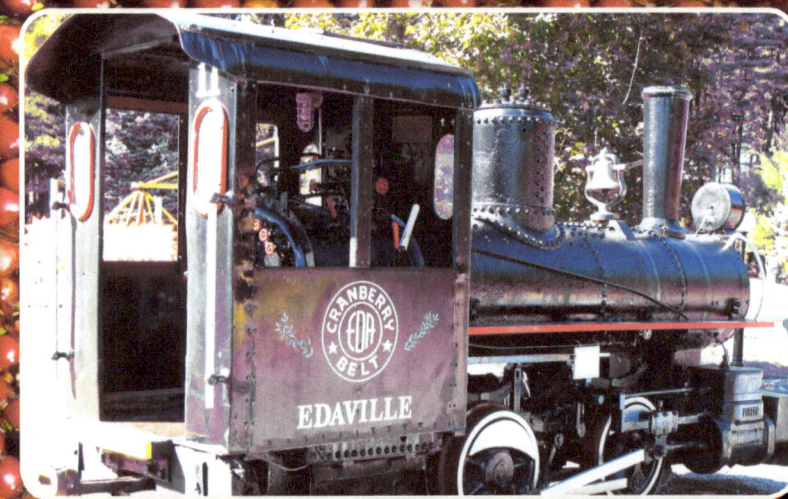

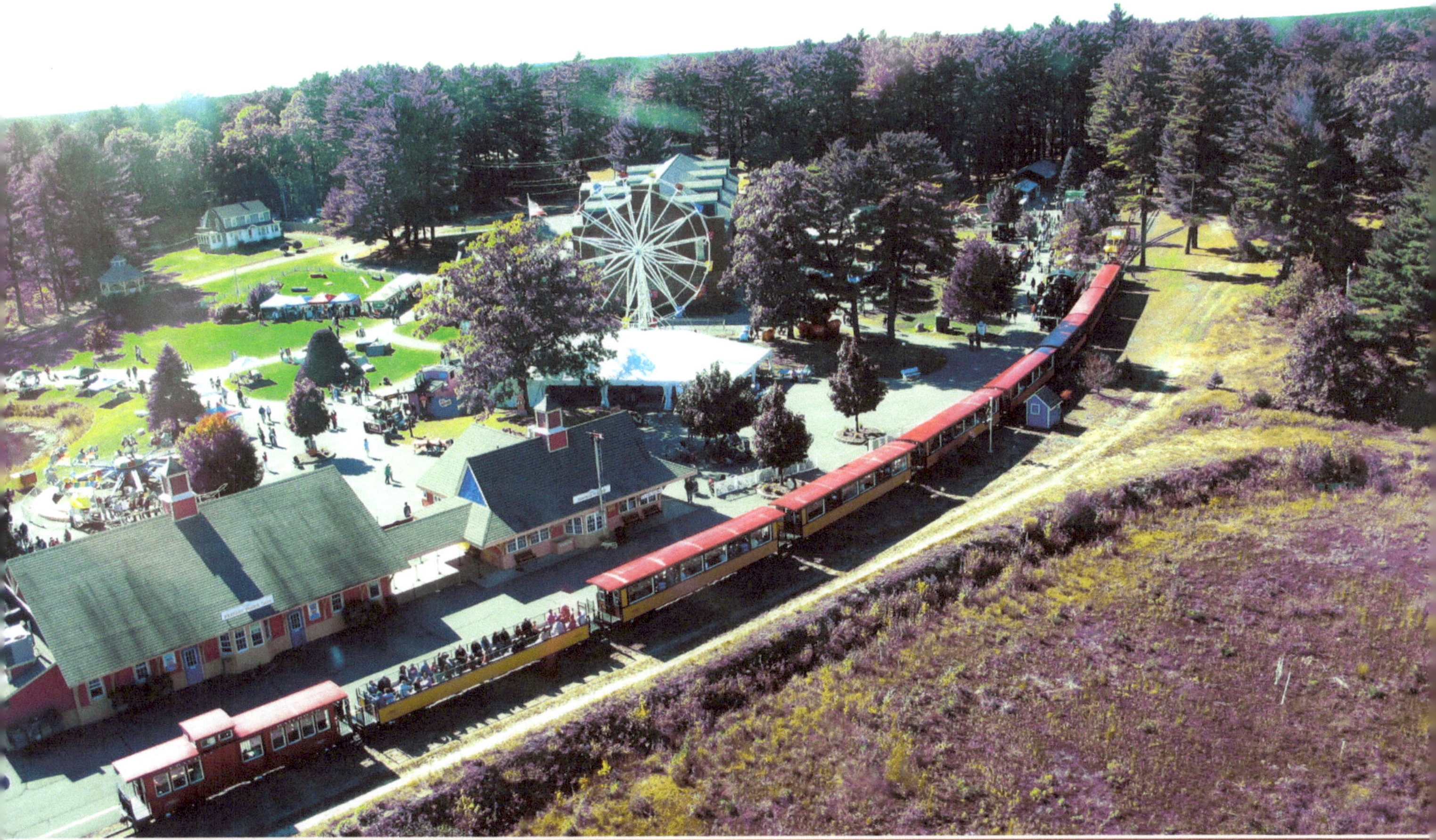

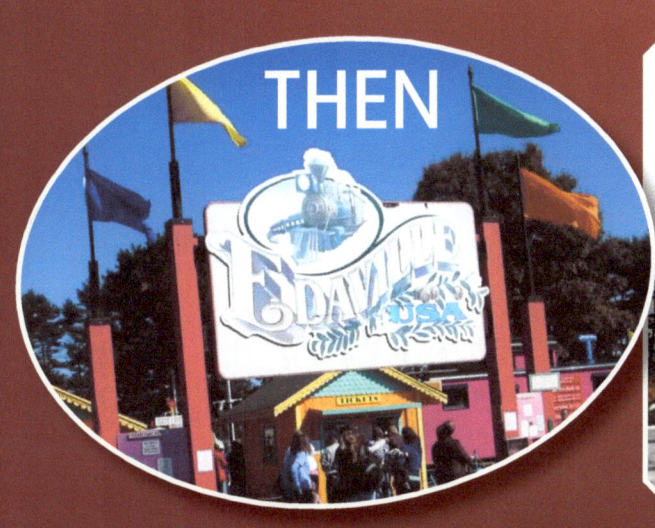

THEN

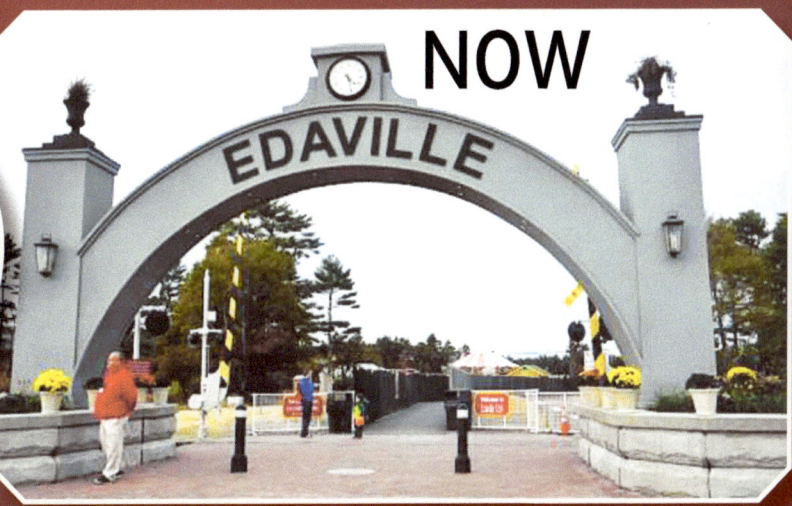

NOW

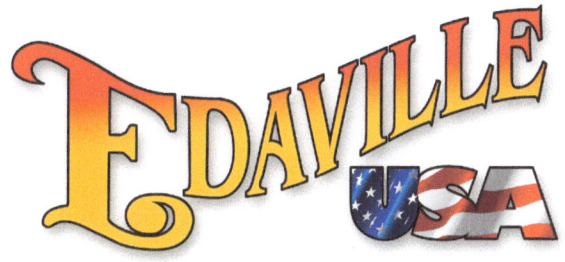

www.Edaville.com